MG 8.2 2pts.

Franklin Delano Roosevelt

Read These Other
Ferguson Career Biographies

Maya Angelou
Author and
Documentary Filmmaker
by Lucia Raatma

Leonard Bernstein
Composer and Conductor
by Jean F. Blashfield

Shirley Temple Black
Actor and Diplomat
by Jean F. Blashfield

George Bush
Business Executive
and U.S. President
by Robert Green

Bill Gates
Computer Programmer
and Entrepreneur
by Lucia Raatma

John Glenn
Astronaut and U.S. Senator
by Robert Green

Martin Luther King Jr.
Minister and
Civil Rights Activist
by Brendan January

Charles Lindbergh
Pilot
by Lucia Raatma

Sandra Day O'Connor
Lawyer and
Supreme Court Justice
by Jean Kinney Williams

Wilma Rudolph
Athlete and Educator
by Alice K. Flanagan

Franklin Delano Roosevelt

U.S. President

ROBERT GREEN

Ferguson Publishing Company
Chicago, Illinois

Photographs ©: AP/Wide World Photos, 86; Archive Photos, 39, 42, 92, 96, 102; Corbis, cover, 34, 36, 46, 66; Franklin D. Roosevelt Library Digital Archives, 8, 13, 15, 19, 26, 28, 31, 44, 49, 52, 55, 58, 61, 64, 69, 72, 75, 78, 82, 89, 100, 105, 108; Liaison Agency/Hulton Getty, 23, 94.

An Editorial Directions Book
Library of Congress Cataloging-in-Publication Data
Green, Robert, 1969–

 Franklin Delano Roosevelt / by Robert Green.
 p. cm.—(Ferguson career biography)
 "An Editorial Directions book"—T.p. verso.
 Includes bibliographical references and index.
 ISBN 0-89434-373-4
 1. Roosevelt, Franklin D. (Franklin Delano), 1882–1945—Juvenile literature. 2. Presidents—United States—Biography—Juvenile literature. [1. Roosevelt, Franklin D. (Franklin Delano), 1882–1945. 2. Presidents.] I. Title. II. Series.

E807 .G694 2001
973.917'092—dc21
[B]   00-048465

Copyright © 2001 by Ferguson Publishing Company
Published and distributed by
Ferguson Publishing Company
200 West Jackson Boulevard, Suite 700
Chicago, Illinois 60606
www.fergpubco.com

Printed in the United States of America
Y-3

CONTENTS

Franklin Delano Roosevelt

Franklin Delano Roosevelt's inauguration in 1933. In his speech, he gave the nation hope in overcoming the Great Depression.

FREEDOM FROM FEAR

On the chilly Saturday morning of March 4, 1933, an open car drove two somber-faced men toward the United States Capitol in Washington, D.C. The shorter man was President Herbert Hoover, whose name had been given to the shantytowns, known as Hoovervilles, that housed a growing number of homeless Americans in cities across the country. Through little fault of his own, President Hoover had become the face of the Great Depression—an economic crisis that had put one-third of the nation's workers out of a job.

The taller man was Franklin Delano Roosevelt, soon to become the thirty-second president of the United States. The car proceeded through the throngs of spectators who had gathered to hear Roosevelt's inaugural speech—his first address to the nation. Roosevelt had been elected president in November 1932. The people who elected him hoped he would get rid of the Hoovervilles and put Americans back to work.

At the Capitol, the two men climbed onto a platform bedecked with festive garlands. Roosevelt made his way to the podium with the help of his son, James, because he could not walk alone. After taking the oath of office, Roosevelt clutched the podium to steady himself on his lifeless legs, which were supported by steel braces. He was about to speak to the people of a nation that had been destroyed financially—people who were wracked with fear about the future.

"First of all," Roosevelt said, "let me assert my firm belief that the only thing we have to fear is fear itself—nameless, unreasoning, unjustified terror which paralyzes needed efforts to convert retreat into advance." Speakers amplified his words for the more than 100,000 people who had gathered to hear the inaugural address. Radio towers carried the speech to millions of other listeners. It was the first time Americans had heard a president's inaugural address on the radio.

Not since the Civil War had the United States been so close to coming apart at the seams. And perhaps never before had Americans felt so low, so helpless, and so paralyzed. Roosevelt well understood the frustrating feelings of paralysis. When he was thirty-nine years old, he had lost the use of his legs—permanently—as a result of the disease known as polio. Roosevelt had struggled to overcome his own sense of weakness and uselessness, and now he had achieved the presidency.

By electing him as their president, Americans were asking him to carry the full weight of the national economic crisis on his shoulders. This smiling man, who gave an impression of great strength despite his weakened body, accepted willingly. "For the trust reposed in me I will return the courage and the devotion that befit the time," he said. "I can do no less."

Charmed Youth

Roosevelt had deep sympathy for the sufferings of Americans during the Great Depression, but these feelings did not result from his own life experience. His childhood was as happy as any boy's in America. "What rivets the reader's attention," commented one historian on a memoir of Franklin's childhood written by his mother, "is the almost complete lack of unhappiness and anxiety in Franklin's life."

Franklin Delano Roosevelt was born on January 30, 1882, at his family's home in Hyde Park, New York. The Roosevelt family home sat on a majestic spot overlooking the Hudson River, which flowed to New York City and the Atlantic Ocean. Hundreds of acres of the family estate, known as Springwood, surrounded the house. With its rolling hills, dappled light, and spectacular views, the Hudson River Valley was celebrated as an American Eden by painters of the Hudson Valley School.

On his father's side, Roosevelt could trace his ancestry back to the earliest Dutch settlers, who had colonized New York City and named it New Amsterdam, after Holland's great trading city. *Roosevelt* is a Dutch name, meaning "field of roses."

Franklin's father, James Roosevelt, was a country squire who maintained the estate by farming and breeding animals. One of his ancestors, Isaac Roo-

Roosevelt as a boy. His mother kept his hair long for the first few years of his life.

sevelt, had served in the Continental Congress and helped finance the Revolutionary War against the British.

James's first wife died, leaving a son named James Roosevelt Roosevelt. This child was born twenty-eight years before his half-brother, Franklin. Sara Delano, James's second wife and Franklin's mother, was also born into a distinguished New York family. Her family had made some of its money in the American clipper-ship trade with China. For two years, Sara lived in Hong Kong where her father ran the family shipping firm.

Franklin adored his parents, who doted on him. His father played the role of the lovable uncle while his mother ran the household. Following the fashions of the times, she dressed young Roosevelt in gowns and kept his hair long for his first few years.

Franklin's life revolved around the household, where he was educated until age fourteen. He led a carefree existence at Springwood. He roamed the estate hunting birds, which he then learned to stuff and mount for display in the house. By the time he entered college, he had collected about 300 species. When the weather was bad, he spent hours poring over his stamp collection in front of the fireplace.

His family spent summers in their home on Campobello Island off the coast of New Brunswick, Canada. There, Franklin lounged on the wide porches, scampered all over the island, and was attended by servants. He learned to sail in the Bay of Fundy, off the coast of Campobello. Boats caught his fancy, and, by the time he was fourteen,

At Hyde Park with his parents. Young Roosevelt enjoyed the time he spent on the family estate.

Franklin had rigged out his own tiny boats and captained them alone. Occasionally, the family traveled to Europe in the summer, visiting historic sites to round out Franklin's education as a gentleman.

Throughout his upbringing, Franklin was taught to behave with noblesse oblige—the sense of honor, generosity, and responsibility that comes with being a member of a privileged family. He was taught to be polite to others and never to look down on people less fortunate than himself. He was taught that he owed a debt of service to society.

A Wider World

Franklin left the small and sheltered world of his home and family for the first time in 1896 when he entered the Groton School in Connecticut at age fourteen. The Groton School was an elite preparatory school for the sons of prominent Americans. Modeled after the British private schools for boys, Groton expected much from its students, both in and out of the classroom.

The headmaster, Reverend Endicott Peabody, was a strict Episcopalian who preached the same sense of social obligation that Franklin had learned from his parents. Peabody was shaping his students for service to society. "If some Groton boys," he said, "do not enter political life and do something for our land, it won't be because they have not been urged."

Franklin was two years older than his classmates when he entered the school, so they regarded him with some suspicion. Some of the other students once made him dance a jig while they slashed at his ankles with hockey sticks.

Trying to overcome the stigma of being a late-comer, Franklin threw himself into many activities. He tried out for baseball, football, and several other sports. The only one he excelled at was the high kick, which required leaping high into the air to kick a pan suspended from the ceiling. Franklin grew 7 inches (18 centimeters) taller while attending Groton, and the added height helped him master the sport. His record kick was 7 feet 3 1/2 inches (2.2 meters).

Although he was never really a great sportsman, Franklin won acceptance from his classmates. He was excellent at debating, and he was generally thought to be clever and compassionate. The young man had his mother's long, straight nose, and he would look down it dramatically during debates as he threw his head back to make his point.

Franklin's popularity also got a boost when his distant cousin, Theodore Roosevelt, a rising young politician and friend of Reverend Peabody's, spoke at the school. Theodore, known as Teddy, was a bundle of energy, ferocity, and humor. His bristling mustache, enormous teeth, and tales of his exciting work as the head of the New York City police board captured the boys' imagination. Teddy told stories about New York City neighborhoods and the crimes he tried to solve and prevent. To Franklin, and to many of the other boys, this outspoken politician and adventurer was a walking, talking storybook hero.

In 1900, Franklin graduated from Groton, winning the Latin prize, a forty-volume set of Shakespeare's works. That year, he enrolled as a freshman at Harvard College in Cambridge, Massachusetts—the oldest of all the American colleges. He and a classmate from Groton, who was also attending Harvard, found an apartment that was close enough to campus that Franklin could walk to class.

At the Groton School. After graduating, Roosevelt went on to Harvard.

Crimson Ink

Classes at Groton School were designed to prepare boys for the prestigious Ivy League colleges of the northeastern United States, of which Harvard was one. Life at Harvard, however, was much less rigid than it had been at Groton. The young men attending the college were free to make their own choices and structure their own lives.

Roosevelt settled into rooms on Mount Auburn Street, the area preferred by many of the wealthier students at Harvard. The fashionable Cambridge, Massachusetts, neighborhood was referred to as the Gold Coast. Roosevelt enjoyed the social setting, which he shared with several Groton graduates and other privileged young men.

Striving to be more like his athletic cousin Teddy, Franklin once again tried out for sports. The disappointing experiences at Groton were repeated, however, and Franklin had to look elsewhere to make his mark.

He found his opportunity at the *Crimson*, the most famous college newspaper in the United States. Franklin threw himself into newspaper work with all his heart. Unlike sports, journalism did not require great physical ability. It also suited young

Roosevelt's temperament—his great determination, his ability to see things through, and his careful attention to detail.

Franklin's work at the *Crimson* consumed more time than his studies did. He worked in the paper's office for up to six hours a day. His hard work allowed him to move "up the ladder" at the paper—but so did his connection to Teddy Roosevelt.

A news reporter is obsessed with getting a "scoop"—being the first reporter to get a piece of important news. Franklin's cousin Teddy was staying in Boston as the guest of Professor Abbott Lowell of Harvard. Franklin discovered that Teddy was planning to give a speech. By that time, Teddy was a figure of national stature, and the speech had not yet been announced for fear of drawing large crowds.

The next day, Franklin announced the upcoming speech on the front page of the *Crimson*, delighted at being the first to break the news. Although Professor Lowell was furious that Franklin would use his family connections in such a way, Teddy was pleased at Franklin's success. The incident further improved Franklin's status at the paper.

Although Franklin completed his schoolwork in

three years, he stayed on for a fourth year to be the newspaper's editor in chief. For the first time in his life, Franklin had snatched the top job. He delighted in the job and the position. He took to wearing suits from Brooks Brothers and pince-nez—tiny spectacles that clip onto the bridge of the nose. Franklin spent a delightful fourth year at Harvard, socializing and running the *Crimson*.

Of course, it helped his newspaper work that Teddy continued to supply him with news from the White House. During Franklin's time at Harvard, Teddy had been elected vice president of the United States under President William McKinley. And when McKinley was assassinated in 1901, Teddy became president.

There was much for Franklin to admire in his cousin. Teddy Roosevelt had organized a group of cowboys from the West and horse-loving gentlemen from the East to form the famous Rough Riders. He personally led these men into battle in Cuba during the Spanish-American War (1898). He had also shown great bravery in combat and fought against tyranny wherever he found it.

More than anything, Teddy Roosevelt hated corruption, and he became known as a reformer.

A famous cousin. Teddy Roosevelt was known for leading the Rough Riders.

His work as president of New York's Board of Police Commissioners had given him an understanding of urban life and problems, yet he also understood the rugged, independent ways of the American West. Teddy was a maverick, little concerned with criticism from anyone. He dismissed the press as a bunch of "muckrakers," reporters who were snooping through people's lives hoping to find scandal.

Franklin thought it was good fun being a muckraker, but he soon began to feel part of a much greater game. The sense of obligation that his parents had instilled ran strong in him. Now, with a member of the family in the White House, Franklin began to have ambitions of his own. He started to imagine himself as another great Roosevelt, another leader of the nation. His political dreaming was put on hold for a while, however, while Franklin pursued another dream.

Eleanor

During his summer breaks from Harvard, Franklin joined in the social whirl of parties and dinners in New York City and Dutchess County. In the process, Franklin had grown close to a tall, wispy girl named

Eleanor. He and Anna Eleanor Roosevelt were not strangers though. She was a distant cousin, and he had known her all his life.

Eleanor was the daughter of Teddy Roosevelt's brother and a member of the Oyster Bay Roosevelts of Long Island, New York—a branch of the family that was even richer than the Roosevelts of Hyde Park. Like Franklin, Eleanor was raised in Dutchess County, but her childhood had been nothing like Franklin's.

When Eleanor was eight years old, her mother died. When she was ten, her father died from the effects of a life of drinking alcohol. Eleanor was raised by her grandmother, who terrified her.

Eleanor's tall and willowy figure, luxuriant hair, and sharp, gray eyes caught Franklin's attention. He saw that this woman, who described herself as an "ugly duckling," was not only beautiful but remarkably intelligent. Eleanor was flattered by the interest of the handsome young Harvard man, and by 1903, they were engaged to be married.

Franklin kept his mother in the dark about his interest in Eleanor. "His mother never did quite know how Franklin managed to carry out his wooing without her getting wind of it," remarked one friend.

On her wedding day. Eleanor and Franklin Roosevelt were married on March 17, 1905.

Despite his mother's concern about the couple's youth, Franklin and Eleanor were married on St. Patrick's Day in 1905, one year after Franklin's Harvard commencement. The ceremony was performed by Reverend Peabody, the headmaster of Groton. And walking down the aisle to give away his niece was the swaggering, toothy-grinned President Theodore Roosevelt, the young groom's idol.

In his Albany office. Senator Roosevelt worked hard in serving the people of New York.

MAN ABOUT TOWN

Franklin's mother had always hoped that Franklin would take a law degree after graduating from Harvard and set up a practice as a gentleman lawyer. She believed that law was one of the few professions that could offer a young aristocrat like Franklin an elite social circle and easy working hours. So in January 1905, Franklin enrolled at Columbia University's law school in New York City.

Franklin found his law studies a bit dull. He longed to get out into the world on his own. In 1907, he passed the New York State bar examination, left Columbia without receiving his degree, and landed a job at the law firm of Carter, Ledyard, and Milburn. With his famous name—his cousin Teddy Roosevelt was still in the White House—Franklin was an attractive catch for the Wall Street firm. The partners hoped Franklin would bring in members of his prestigious social circle as new clients.

New York City was a good place for a young man just starting out. Roosevelt had the means to make the social rounds, and he and Eleanor lived in a luxurious townhouse on East Sixty-Fifth Street in Manhattan, which his mother had built for them. Unfortunately for Eleanor, however, Franklin's mother moved into the house next door and connected the two dwellings with an interior passageway.

Franklin's father had died while Franklin was attending Harvard. Since then, Sara Roosevelt had doted on her son. Her constant attention made life difficult for Eleanor, however. While young Roosevelt was at the office or dining with colleagues, Eleanor was left alone with Franklin's domineering mother.

Joys and Sorrows

Eleanor's life improved somewhat when she gave birth to Anna Roosevelt in 1906. She now had her own child to fuss over. A son, James, was born in 1907. Franklin's life seemed to be progressing smoothly, and he was having a good time. He had flexible hours, worked with like-minded socialites, and spent much of his time playing cards. The first real tragedy of Franklin's life, however, cast a shadow over his frivolous New York existence.

Mother and daughter. The Roosevelts were happy to welcome Anna to their family.

In 1909, the Roosevelts' third child, Franklin Delano Jr., died at the age of eighteen months. For the first time in his life, Franklin faced absolute misery.

To make matters worse, he began to feel that his budding professional life was meaningless. The idea of practicing corporate law—handling endless paperwork and meeting with clients about petty disputes—left him unsatisfied. He was bored and, more important, he felt that he was not living up to the ideals of public service instilled in him as a child.

Public Service

Fortunately, the Democratic Party had plans for Franklin. In 1910, he was asked to run for a seat in the New York State Senate for the Twenty-Sixth District, which included his hometown of Hyde Park in Dutchess County. The offer was like a miracle cure for Franklin. Despite his mother's disapproval, he accepted the offer with enthusiasm. Hadn't he been taught that he had an obligation to do some good for society? Hadn't his cousin Teddy brought honor to the profession of politics, which Franklin's mother considered unfit for a gentleman?

Although he had voted for Teddy, who was a

Republican, Franklin identified with the Democratic Party. In truth, however, there was not much difference between the two parties' views. Both considered themselves "progressives," the then-fashionable term for people who felt that dishonest politicians should be put out of office. Teddy Roosevelt called these corrupt men "malefactors" and fought against them in the name of the people. Franklin shared his cousin's views.

The Campaign Trail

Both Roosevelt politicians had the advantage of having money. They could finance their own campaigns. Any attempted bribes would have been peanuts compared to their own bank accounts. But Franklin's money and good breeding were both advantages and disadvantages.

Democratic leaders were happy that Roosevelt could finance his own campaign. However, they were also worried about how the people of Dutchess County would react. How many candidates owned an estate and rode around the countryside on horseback?

"The idea of a rich young patrician in politics was unfamiliar," wrote historian Finis Farr, "and

Shaking many hands. Roosevelt enjoyed meeting people when he campaigned in New York State.

County Chairman Edward E. Perkins warned that Franklin's manner might be taken as supercilious [proud] by ordinary men. The elders were bothered by the gold-rimmed pince-nez, the tossing back of the head, and the ready laugh which did not quite ring true."

As it turned out, Franklin took to campaigning like a natural. More than anything, he loved talking

Franklin Delano Roosevelt: U.S. President

to people. He drove around the counties in a red convertible, making speeches and meeting the locals. On one occasion, he crossed the state line into Connecticut, delivered a speech, and drove away—never realizing that he had been talking to people who couldn't vote for him even if they wanted to. No matter, Franklin was now free from the stifling world of the law firm, and he was having a grand time.

Senator Roosevelt

Roosevelt won the election of 1910 and took his seat in the state legislature in Albany, the capital of New York. He rented an elegant house not far from the capitol.

Franklin was something of a curiosity in the legislature. His humorous manner, his famous name, and his great wealth set him apart from many of the other legislators, some of whom were just scraping by on their government salaries. Roosevelt also frowned on the dishonest backroom dealings and lack of principles he found among many New York politicians.

Although Franklin had enjoyed living in New York City, he felt separate from the city's politicians

As senator, Roosevelt served in the New York State senate from 1910 to 1913.

and the great political "machine"—or organization—that put them in office. That machine, which was known as Tammany Hall, was controlled by Democratic Party leaders called "bosses." These men decided who would run for office and who would be supported by the party. Roosevelt thought this practice was tyranny of the worst sort because it often ignored the wishes of the voters. Tammany Hall was also marked by corruption, which eventually led to criminal charges against some of its members.

Early on, Franklin set himself apart from the machine. In 1911, he opposed the Tammany Hall appointment of William Sheehan for the U.S. Senate. At that time, U.S. senators were appointed by state legislators rather than elected, as they are today. Roosevelt thought the appointment of Sheehan reeked of "bossism." He drew support from other dissatisfied Democrats and won national attention for exposing the corruption of his party. In the end, Sheehan was pulled out of the running—although Tammany Hall selected his replacement.

Roosevelt's straight shooting marked him as a man of integrity and won the notice of politicians beyond New York. His principles matched his progressive ambitions.

Franklin was just as hardworking as a legislator as he had been as an editor for the *Crimson* at Harvard. He worked on bills for soil conservation, the right of women to vote, worker's compensation, and—in opposition to Tammany Hall—a bill that would allow the people of New York State to elect their own candidates to the U.S. Senate.

On to Washington

In 1912, Roosevelt supported a candidate in the Democratic presidential primary who shared his own thinking. That candidate was the Democratic governor of New Jersey, Woodrow Wilson. Tammany Hall considered Wilson an uptight moralizer and backed another candidate, however.

Like Franklin, Wilson believed in progressive ideals. He was an academic and one-time head of Princeton University. He was also devoted to the reformist platform that Franklin was fighting for in New York and, like Franklin, he was above any hint of corruption.

Wilson won the primary—and the presidency. Roosevelt's opposition to Tammany Hall and his sup-

President Woodrow Wilson. Roosevelt served as assistant secretary of the navy during Wilson's administration.

port of Wilson were rewarded by a post in the new administration. In 1913, Roosevelt became assistant secretary of the navy. The boy who had loved sailboats found himself, at age thirty-one, in charge of an entire fleet of American warships.

Like Teddy Roosevelt, who had held that post before him, Franklin argued for a larger fleet. He made a hobby of studying naval history and believed that the United States must be prepared to protect its interests throughout the world.

World War I

When Austria-Hungary attacked its European neighbors in 1914, launching World War I, the need for a larger fleet became more urgent. The United States began sending supplies to Britain and France along shipping routes in the Atlantic. The convoys were protected by U.S. warships.

The United States was not eager to intervene in a European war, but as the war engulfed the continent, America increased its aid to Britain. German submarines called U-boats circled the British Isles and destroyed ships that were attempting to supply the British. The U-boats also sank American ships even though the United States was not in the war. In 1917, the United States finally responded by entering the war and sent American troops to Europe. Roosevelt threw himself into the war effort, and even visited the front lines of battle in France and Belgium.

In 1918, the war ended. American servicemen sailed home, leaving behind a continent devastated by war. Even the victors—the British and the French—were financially ruined by the war. "The beneficiary was the United States," wrote historian Paul Fussell, "which emerged an undisputed Great Power by virtue of manufacturing and shipping material. Indeed, the United States, as historian Marc Ferro observes 'could rightly be considered the only victor of the war, since their territory was intact, and they became creditors of all the other belligerents.'"

The League of Nations

In 1919, President Wilson and other world leaders attended a peace conference held in a palace at Versailles just outside of Paris, the capital of France. As a representative of the Navy Department, Roosevelt observed the peace conference. At the conference, an international body was created to settle disputes between nations. It was hoped that this new body, called the League of Nations, would prevent future world wars through the reasoned voices of international diplomats.

After the war, however, Americans wanted to hear no more of foreign affairs. The people of the United States receded from the world stage, like a turtle ducking back into its shell. Wilson had warned

Trying for world peace. British Prime Minister David Lloyd George (left), French Prime Minister Georges Clemenceau (center), and President Woodrow Wilson attended the peace conference at Versailles.

against this kind of isolationism. He did not want to see the United States withdraw from the larger world. He believed that Americans could provide a moral compass to guide other nations. Many Americans feared that, instead of preventing war, the League would draw the United States into more foreign conflicts.

Roosevelt, however, became an outspoken supporter of the League of Nations. In 1920, he made the case for the League as the vice-presidential candidate on a ticket with James M. Cox of Ohio. Cox had selected Roosevelt as his running mate because of Franklin's growing influence in national politics, his famous name, and his ability to balance the ticket geographically. A distinguished Northeasterner like Roosevelt, Cox thought, would help the Ohio politician broaden his support within the country.

Back on the Campaign Trail

Franklin and Eleanor set out on a grueling tour of the United States. Women had gained the right to vote in 1920, and Eleanor became one of the first American women to campaign with her husband in an attempt to encourage women to vote.

Touring the country. Eleanor Roosevelt joined her husband and his staff in the 1920 campaign.

At every stop, Roosevelt tried to argue, persuade, and tease Americans into a more global outlook. He was determined to win support for the League. President Wilson also campaigned for the League on his return from France.

As Roosevelt toured the country, however, his health began to fail. The more exhausted he became, the more he refused to compromise on the League. He demanded that all the terms of the League be accepted as they were. After just three weeks of campaigning, Roosevelt collapsed.

Disillusioned with Wilson, World War I, and the League of Nations, Americans voted overwhelmingly for a Republican administration in 1920. Congress voted not to sign the Treaty of Versailles and abandoned the League. In later years, the United States would join the League's successor—the United Nations—but in 1920, the idea was resoundingly rejected. For the first time in nearly a decade, Franklin Roosevelt found himself out of a government job.

At Warm Springs, Georgia. Roosevelt and his family spent much time at their home in this resort.

HARD TIMES

3

The prosperous 1920s—an era known as the Roaring Twenties—was a good time for Franklin to return to private enterprise. He formed his own law firm in New York City and became the vice president of Fidelity and Deposit Company of Maryland, an investment bonding company. The money was good but, as usual, Roosevelt was not interested in his income.

The return to private life had other advantages for Roosevelt, however. He once again had an ordered family life with time for vacationing and leisure. He attended dinner parties in the hotels of New York City, spent part of the year at Hyde Park, and summered at Campobello.

In August 1921, on one of his annual trips to the Campobello summer house, Roosevelt was fishing off the deck of a friend's yacht, the *Sabalo*. Few things made Franklin as happy as tramping around a ship, fixing lines, hoisting sails, and losing himself in the many chores required aboard a boat. While Roosevelt was walking across the decks of the *Sabalo*, he slipped on some fish blood. With a great splash, the former assistant secretary of the Navy plunged into the chilly waters of the Bay of Fundy.

Roosevelt, who had been swimming in those waters since childhood, thought nothing of the accident. By dinnertime the next evening, however, he felt ill. His legs throbbed, and he was tired and feverish. Within a few days, Roosevelt was wracked with chills and unable to walk. He had contracted a disease called infantile paralysis, poliomyelitis, or polio.

As he was carried away from Campobello on a stretcher to a launch headed for the mainland, Roosevelt waved and smiled to his eight-year-old son,

Summering at Campobello. Roosevelt joined his family and friends for many summers near the shore.

Franklin Jr., his fourth son who was named the same as the boy who died. "I decided Dad couldn't be so sick after all if he could wave and smile," the grown boy remembered years later.

Today, American children are routinely vaccinated against polio. As a result, the disease is no longer of much concern to Americans. At that time, however, it was a dreaded illness. There was no vaccine and no definite cure. Roosevelt's legs were permanently paralyzed, and he was forced to learn to live without the use of them.

An Invisible Enemy

In his townhouse in New York City, Roosevelt got used to moving about in a wheelchair. To get himself into bed, he used a series of hand straps, hoisting himself from the chair onto the mattress. As the months passed, the intense exercise developed the muscles of his upper body. As his thin frame filled out, his appearance changed into that of a strong middle-aged man.

He grappled with pain on a daily basis, as the muscles and tendons in his legs contracted and had to be forced to stretch again. If he did not continue to stretch the muscles, Roosevelt would be forced to remain in his wheelchair permanently—and sleep there too. The thought was unbearable, so he endured the many painful exercises required.

Although he was fighting depression along with his physical limitations, Roosevelt presented a good face to the world. He refused to become an invalid and, instead, would often throw his head back with his usual boisterous laugh—a great effort that often shocked visitors. Sometimes he would try to impress a guest by climbing out of one chair, crawling across the floor—by pulling himself by his arms—and lifting himself into another chair. Few visitors were unmoved by Roosevelt's cheerfulness as he performed this torturous feat.

Warm Springs

In 1924, George Foster Peabody, a banker friend of Roosevelt's, suggested that Franklin take a trip to his resort at Warm Springs, Georgia. There, Roosevelt could bathe in the natural mineral baths that bubbled up from underground. Peabody told him of the healing effects of the baths on another victim of polio, and Roosevelt accepted enthusiastically.

The heat of the waters and their high mineral content worked wonders on Roosevelt's legs. The baths not only eased his movement, but also eased the psychological pain. In water, Roosevelt still had a sense of mobility. He merrily splashed about, smiling and joking. He felt a sense of optimism that he had not felt since the illness first struck. His spirits were lifted as his body floated in the soothing waters.

Healing waters. The effects of Roosevelt's polio were improved in Warm Springs.

Roosevelt became so interested in the healing powers of the waters that he took over running the resort. In 1927, he established the Georgia Warm Springs Foundation for other polio sufferers. Roosevelt swam around the pools chatting with the other polio victims and listening to their stories. He was glad to meet people in a situation similar to his, and he developed a deep sympathy for the suffering of others. His close attention to the other patients earned him the nickname "Dr. Roosevelt."

Roosevelt spent nearly three-quarters of his personal fortune establishing the resort, and he opened it to anyone suffering from polio. For the rest of his life, he spent several months a year at Warm Springs.

On his trips south to the springs, Roosevelt frequently stopped off in Washington, D.C., to keep a finger on the political pulse of the nation. His mother had insisted that Roosevelt should take it easy, but he hated sitting idly in his wheelchair. He longed to get back into the game.

Eleanor was his greatest supporter, helping him get through the darkest days and reminding him that he still had the stuff of a great political leader. Louis Howe, a former newsman who had been with Roosevelt since he ran for the New York State Senate, was also a help to him. Like Eleanor, Howe encouraged Roosevelt to reenter politics. The only question was: Would the voters elect a man in a wheelchair?

Governor of the Empire State

Roosevelt received an invitation to speak at the Democratic convention for the presidential primary of 1928. The candidate was Al Smith, who became known as the Happy Warrior. Smith was a Tammany Hall man, a populist, and a Catholic.

Roosevelt overlooked his own dislike for Tammany and praised Smith in his speech at the convention. Smith was chosen as the Democratic candidate in the general election.

Smith was a city politician, familiar with the wheeling and dealing of big city politics. Also, he had supporters among the Irish and other minorities. He opposed prohibition—laws forbidding the sale of alcohol that were unpopular in New York City.

Al Smith knew his views were not popular in other parts of the country, however. Many Americans, especially in the Midwest, were in favor of prohibition and wouldn't dream of voting for a Catholic anyway. Smith turned to Roosevelt for one more favor. He asked Roosevelt to run for governor of New York to give the Democratic ticket a name with national prominence.

Good friends. Al Smith (standing) encouraged Roosevelt to run for the office of governor.

Roosevelt needed a great deal of persuading. He didn't feel physically able to campaign and also he wasn't sure he would win because Republicans were gaining votes all over the country. But Smith was a persuasive man. "I need you, Frank," he said to Roosevelt during one phone call. "It all depends on you."

Roosevelt announced his candidacy—and immediately set out to conquer the problems of campaigning. Louis Howe devised ways to avoid publicity when Roosevelt was climbing in and out of his wheelchair. When he delivered speeches, Franklin would stand, resting on the lectern, his legs held stiff by braces.

In addition, Franklin ordered a Packard Twelve car, modified so that it could be driven by hand controls. He drove around the state looking fit and full of vigor. He greeted people while seated in his car and chatted with an arm hanging over the side. He had a marvelous smile, his voice rang with confidence, and he looked every inch a winner.

When the 1928 election counts were in, Smith had suffered a brutal defeat by Republican Herbert Hoover. In fact, the Republicans had gained all over the country—not just winning the presidency, but also gaining seats in Congress and other offices in the states. The one notable exception to the widespread Republican victory was the election of Democratic Governor Franklin D. Roosevelt in New York.

Fighting for Reform

Roosevelt had his work cut out for him in Albany. Republicans held the majority in the New York legislature and vowed to oppose the new governor, who did not share their views about government.

Roosevelt believed that government could bring about social change. He felt that laws could improve the average man's life—a belief he held throughout his political life. The Republicans, on the other hand, thought the government should not intrude in people's lives or in the economy unless it was necessary. They believed that the government was just as likely to ruin a good situation as to fix a bad one.

His strong personality and mastery of the political process enabled Roosevelt to succeed in gaining support for his reforms. He passed bills to reforest parts of New York State and conserve wilderness areas. He passed bills for pensions that would help the elderly pay their bills when they were too old to

Governor Roosevelt. While in office, he fought to preserve the environment and improve the lives of average people.

Franklin Delano Roosevelt: U.S. President

work. He regulated working hours for women and children and fought for higher wages for laborers.

Times were still good in the late 1920s when Franklin was fighting for these reforms. There was money to be made, and it was easy money. The stock market did a brisk trade, as wealthy Americans bought and sold shares of publicly owned companies. Jazz music played in nightclubs across the country, and people created exciting new dances to accompany the new rhythms. Women cut their hair into short bobs, and they smoked cigarettes in public for the first time. The 1920s became known as the Jazz Age, a happy-go-lucky period that author F. Scott Fitzgerald wrote about in books such as *The Great Gatsby*. The characters in his stories were wealthy socialites whose main concern was which party they would attend next. These were not the concerns of the average person, who had to work to make ends meet even in the best of times.

Before becoming governor, Roosevelt would have fit right in with these bright young people of New York society. Now, in public office, he had to worry about the citizens who were not as fortunate as these wealthy few. These boom years really benefited only a small part of society.

Black Thursday

The Jazz Age came to an abrupt end on October 24, 1929—a day known as Black Thursday. A growing sense that the American economy might change for the worse made some people suddenly panic. Their panic set off a record-high selling frenzy in the New York stock market. More than 12 million shares of stock were traded, and prices sank. Millions of dollars were lost.

Some investors lost everything in a single day; some committed suicide. News of the stock-market crash raced across the country.

During the next few months, people crowded into the banks to withdraw their money. Such widespread withdrawals of money are called bank runs. As the banks ran short of money, they were forced to stop lending money, to call in the repayment of loans, and foreclose on houses.

Because of the widespread financial panic, people stopped spending money. As a result, products piled up in warehouses. Many businesses were forced to fire their workers, which made matters worse. The crisis tumbled along, growing ever larger, like a snowball rolling downhill. The entire nation plunged into the darkest economic times in U.S. history.

Black Thursday marked the beginning of the Great Depression. One-third of the nation's workers lost their jobs, and many wandered across the country seeking work wherever they could find it. "As we reached the end of 1931," wrote historian Finis Farr, "hope no longer existed for millions of people.

A warm meal. Roosevelt organized soup kitchens and other programs for those most affected by the Great Depression.

One saw that it was absent from the eyes of the neatly dressed men who came to one's door and asked for any kind of work."

Roosevelt Takes Charge

The depression hit New York State hard too, and Governor Roosevelt quickly took action. This kind of crisis required the type of government involvement that he had always believed in. Acting ahead of the leaders of other states, Roosevelt created a relief plan for New Yorkers. He organized food kitchens to feed the hungry and used state funds to pay for projects that would put people to work.

Roosevelt, who was reelected for a second term as governor in 1930, won the admiration of New Yorkers during the depression. The government had not caused the depression, but Roosevelt believed that the government could do something about it. As the presidential election of 1932 neared, Roosevelt thought he knew what that "something" was.

On July 2, 1932, Roosevelt announced his candidacy for the presidency of the United States. He arrived late at the Democratic convention in Chicago that day because of bad weather. Roosevelt traveled to the convention by airplane, which created quite a stir because flying was still a novelty at that time. After being helped onto the stage, Roosevelt stood at the podium, and his voice rang out clear and strong. "I pledge myself to a New Deal for the American people," he said. And the people believed him.

Hail to the chief. Roosevelt was elected as the thirty-second president of the United States.

THE NEW DEAL

President Hoover privately raged at the possibility of losing an election to the Democrats. The Great Depression was at its lowest point, and the economy had nowhere to go but up. Hoover continued to warn against creating a federal system for handing out money during these hard times. He believed that such a system would sap the working spirit of the country. Not surprisingly, his hard-line approach made him the most hated man in America.

Most of all, Hoover resented having his name attached to the shantytowns—the

Hoovervilles—built by the unemployed and the homeless. Hoover thought this was an unfair blow, but the president—whether he deserves it or not—is always held responsible for the economic welfare of the country. The man at the top is the one in charge.

A Seattle Hooverville. These kinds of shantytowns were named after Herbert Hoover.

The voters reminded Hoover of this fact by electing Franklin Delano Roosevelt as the thirty-second president of the United States. They also elected a Democratic majority to both houses of Congress.

Getting to Work

Roosevelt's New Deal was a radical departure from Hoover's policies. In his first message to the country, the new president promised that the government would find jobs for people. "Our greatest primary task is to put people to work," he said. He spoke of the forgotten man—the honest, hardworking American who, through no fault of his own, found his life in a shambles. Roosevelt made it plain that he did not intend to stand by and wait for the economy to improve while millions of people suffered.

Roosevelt's first act as president was to call an emergency session of Congress, in which he outlined the first steps needed to strengthen the economy. He also spoke personally with the members of Congress to gain their support, which led to a number of new laws.

His first target was the banks. The bank runs, caused by panic, had made a hole in the very fabric of the U.S. economy. Thirty-eight states had closed their banks, cutting off services that were needed for the economy to prosper. Many other banks teetered on the brink of ruin. Roosevelt calmly ordered all banks to close for four days after his inauguration; in this way, he hoped to slow the economic decline.

Congress passed an emergency banking bill—the Emergency Banking Relief Act—which helped support the surviving banks. Eventually, Congress created the Federal Deposit Insurance Corporation (FDIC). Through this system, the federal government insures the money people deposit in their bank accounts. The FDIC is still in place today, to prevent the kind of disastrous bank runs that occurred during the depression.

The Fireside Chats

Roosevelt raised support for his new economic plan—and raised the country's spirits—by speaking to the American people by radio. These "fireside chats" were delivered from his office and broadcast to millions of homes. Television had not yet been invented, and the radio was the best way to reach a large audience.

Talking to the people. Roosevelt became known for his fireside chats, which were broadcast by radio.

If ever a man were born for radio, it was Franklin Roosevelt. He could deliver his talks while seated comfortably, rather than having to climb onto a podium in leg braces. He had a strong, comforting voice. His calm and confident tone made Americans feel they were listening to a good uncle, who was carefully explaining the workings of the government and reassuring them that all would be well.

Roosevelt's first fireside chat explained banking. In plain language, he described how banks worked and where money was kept. "First of all, let me state the simple fact that when you deposit money in a bank, the bank does not put the money into a safe-deposit vault," he said.

It may have been a simple fact for a government official, but some Americans had never known how banks worked. The next day, many people brought the money that they had withdrawn back to the banks. By the end of the week, most banks were open for business again. Grateful listeners to Roosevelt's program had gained new confidence in the banking system.

This was essential, because lack of confidence—or, as Roosevelt had once said, fear itself—had caused the depression to spiral downward. In his fireside chats, Roosevelt was performing one of the essential roles of the president—to instill confidence in the public. "Confidence and courage are the essentials of success in carrying out our plan," he told his listeners.

Democratic and Republican legislators also welcomed this optimism. They matched Roosevelt's enthusiasm by passing a remarkable number of new laws in 1933, during a period that is now known as the Hundred Days.

Changes in the Air

During Roosevelt's presidency, many government-sponsored projects were established to put Americans back to work. In better times, most of these projects would probably never have existed.

The Tennessee Valley Authority (TVA) was created to build dams and power plants that would provide affordable energy in seven states. The TVA employed thousands of laborers. The Civilian Conservation Corps (CCC) put millions of people to work reforesting sections of the country. The Civil Works Administration (CWA) employed 4 million people. The Agricultural Adjustment Administration (AAA) worked to solve the farming crisis, and the National Recovery Administration (NRA) oversaw working conditions and established fair practices for every industry.

As part of his program of reform, Roosevelt signed the law that repealed the Prohibition Act,

Back to work. The Civilian Conservation Corps helped reforest many sections of the country.

making it legal, for the first time in more than a decade, to sell and drink alcohol. The stock market, which had sparked the depression, also caught Roosevelt's sharp eye. To regulate stock trading, Congress established the Securities and Exchange

Commission (SEC), which made small steps toward overseeing the New York Stock Exchange.

Roosevelt's reforms were grand-scale social experiments. Some were outright failures, and some were modest successes, but they all created a new spirit of optimism in a country ravaged by economic depression. Roosevelt had lived up to his promise to use the government as an agent for economic good.

Roosevelt's opponents, however, accused him of trying to control private business and redistribute wealth. When Roosevelt recognized the legitimacy of the communist Soviet Union in 1933, some critics even accused him of being a communist—a person who believes that the state should own everything. Despite what his critics said, however, Roosevelt was not trying to make radical changes in government. He was seeking to right the ship, not turn it upside down.

Workers and the Elderly

Perhaps Roosevelt's two most radical reforms were his efforts to strengthen the position of workers and to establish pensions for elderly people who could no longer earn an income. In 1935, he sponsored the Wagner Act, which set up the National Labor Relations Board (NLRB). The NLRB allowed workers to organize unions and bargain as a group with their employers. Through the unions, workers had a place at the bargaining table for the first time. They used this new bargaining position to get pay raises and other benefits for their members. The labor-union movement created by the Wagner Act has survived to the present day.

Roosevelt addressed the financial problems of the elderly with the Social Security Act of 1935. He believed that the government had an obligation to support the elderly after a lifetime of hard work—and should not let them simply wither away in poverty. The Social Security Act established pensions, which would be paid by the government, to give retired people the money they needed to pay their rent and buy necessities. To some degree, this practice helped stimulate the economy, because it enabled people to buy goods that were previously unaffordable.

Social Security became a permanent feature of the U.S. economy. The system is so popular that politicians who discuss changing it risk ending their careers—but, because it is so expensive for the

MORE SECURITY FOR THE AMERICAN FAMILY

THE WIDOW OF A QUALIFIED WORKER WILL RECEIVE MONTHLY BENEFITS AT AGE 65. IN CERTAIN CASES, AN AGED DEPENDENT PARENT MAY GET BENEFITS. ...

FOR INFORMATION WRITE OR CALL AT THE NEAREST FIELD OFFICE OF THE

SOCIAL SECURITY BOARD

Taking care of the elderly. Roosevelt's administration created Social Security, a fund that provides money for retired citizens.

The New Deal

government to maintain, the program continues to be a subject of debate.

As the election of 1936 neared, Roosevelt's enemies in Congress used his federal-spending programs as ammunition against him. He was attacked as a "class warrior," who was redistributing wealth from the rich to the poor, and paying for it all with taxes.

With so many successes behind him, however, Roosevelt was a confident campaigner. In a speech in Chicago in 1936, he answered those who accused him of destroying private industry: "Today, for the first time in seven years, the banker, the storekeeper, the small factory owner, the industrialist, can all sit back and enjoy the company of their own ledgers," he said. "They are in the black." He reminded his listeners that everyone was better off than they had been before his administration—and that his New Deal programs had begun the nation's recovery.

Roosevelt was reelected in a landslide victory. He headed into four more years in the White House, knowing that he had won the people's confidence.

The WPA

During his second administration, often referred to as the Second New Deal, Roosevelt pressed ahead with his reforms. One project in particular, the Works Progress Administration (WPA), became a shining example of his social experiments. (After 1939, the project was called the Works Projects Administration.)

The WPA put 2 million Americans back to work. It organized people to build roads, hospitals, and schools. Other WPA workers taught children and illiterate adults how to read. WPA bookmobiles traveled across the country, offering everyone the opportunity to read. WPA workers even translated books into braille for the blind.

One of the most controversial WPA projects sponsored artists, writers, and musicians. They were paid with public money to produce their art. Writers wrote guides to every state. Artists painted murals on the walls of schools and federal buildings. Musicians performed plays and concerts across the country. Republican pointed to this project as an example of government excess. "Should the government be employing artists?" they asked. "They have to eat too," Roosevelt replied.

The Republicans in Congress were not just playing politics with a Democratic president. They were asking serious questions about the nature of government and what it should—and could afford—to

Supporting the arts. One of the Works Progress Administration programs gave money to assist musicians, writers, and painters.

do for its citizens. Was Roosevelt starting a danger-ous trend of providing government funds to the unemployed? Would the new laws keep Americans from starting their own enterprises?

These questions caused a shift in the congres-sional elections in Roosevelt's second term. Repub-licans rallied and regained seats in both the House and the Senate. Roosevelt's easy days were behind him. In the late 1930s, he was forced to compromise on many of the bills he put before Congress.

Checks and Balances

The Republican legislators were not Roosevelt's greatest obstacle, however. In 1935, the Supreme Court overturned the National Recovery Act. The Supreme Court is responsible for determining whether laws are in accordance with the Constitu-tion of the United States.

The three branches of the U.S. government are designed to prevent any one branch from becoming too powerful—through a system of checks and bal-ances. In 1935, the Supreme Court exerted its right to "check and balance" the actions of the other two branches: the executive (the president) and the leg-islative (Congress). The Supreme Court ruled that the NRA had taken over the rights of the states. The Court also found that Roosevelt was meddling in the economic life of the country in a way that was not allowed by the Constitution. The Court said that Roosevelt was interfering with the practices of private businesses to conduct their own affairs as they saw fit.

Roosevelt was furious. He believed he was fighting for the good of the country, and he felt it was absurd that the government would try to stop him. He looked at the situation and realized that he needed more support from the Supreme Court. So he asked Congress to allow him to choose six new Supreme Court members—justices who would support his programs.

This request was the worst step of his administration. Even the average person realized the danger of allowing a president to "pack" the Court to his advantage. The Constitution was carefully designed to avoid such an imbalance of power. Congress rejected the president's request by an overwhelming majority.

Despite its flaws, Roosevelt's New Deal went a long way toward restoring confidence in America. It shored up the banking system, created jobs, and jump-started the economy. It did not, however, end the Great Depression. Another kind of crisis would pull the United States out of its financial woes—a world war that would create a demand for American goods all over the globe.

Signing the declaration of war. The United States entered World War II in 1941.

CITIZENS OF THE WORLD

5

While Roosevelt was battling the Great Depression in the United States, the threat of war was growing in other parts of the world. Dictators in Germany, Italy, and Japan were becoming more powerful and more ruthless. Another world war was brewing.

In 1919—at the peace conference in Versailles, France, after World War I—President Woodrow Wilson had fought tirelessly for a fair deal for the Germans. The French and British, however, turned a deaf ear and refused to help Germany repair the crippling damages it had suffered during the war. As a result, Germany plunged into financial and political chaos, and the German people grew desperate. Searching for help, they turned to Adolf Hitler, a failed artist and a disillusioned veteran of World War I. Hitler promised to restore pride to the German people. He was appointed as the chancellor, or leader, of Germany in 1933.

Hitler lived up to his promise to restart the German economy by increasing arms production. German factories pumped out deadly new weapons. Then, in 1936, in violation of the Treaty of Versailles, German soldiers marched into the Rhineland, an area of Germany next to France.

Less than one year earlier, Italian dictator Benito Mussolini, in a first attempt to expand his empire, had invaded the kingdom of Ethiopia in Africa. In 1937, the Japanese emperor Hirohito began his plans to conquer Asia. His troops launched a major attack against China , marching down the coast , and destroying everything in their path. Their methods were ruthless and effective. The small island nation of Japan overcame the great Chinese dragon with remarkable ease.

Watching and Waiting

Roosevelt had seen the battle fronts of World War I firsthand, and he knew well the threat that a rearmed Germany posed. Roosevelt had never agreed with the wave of American isolationism that followed World War I. He watched the growing threat of war with interest and anxiety.

When Germany made its lightning advance into Poland in 1939, Britain and France honored their treaties with Poland and declared war on Germany. Within weeks, German mobile armored divisions climbed through the mountains, sliced through the Netherlands and Belgium, and took over Paris, the French capital.

Americans were stunned. The United States had been sympathetic to the French since the Revolutionary War, when French ships helped supply the colonists. Americans could not imagine Nazis, as the followers of Hitler were called, marching down the boulevards of the romantic city of Paris. Roosevelt was eager to do something, but the country was against becoming involved in another foreign war. He knew that he needed the people's support to win another term as president.

Invasion. German troops marched into France and took over the Paris capital.

Four More Years

As Europe and Asia began their descent into war, Roosevelt was signing the American Neutrality Act, a pledge to keep the United States out of World War II. He had signed it in 1935, hoping to win a third term in 1940. No U.S. president had ever served three terms.

This next presidential campaign proved to be Roosevelt's toughest, however. His Republican opponent, Wendell L. Willkie, a businessman from Indiana, warned the American people that it was dangerous to give any one man the power of the presidency for more than a decade. He crisscrossed the country calling Roosevelt a threat to democracy. In speech after speech, both in person and on the radio, he claimed that Roosevelt would lead the country into war and asked the people to turn him out of office.

For his part, the president boarded the Roosevelt Express and traveled the country reminding people who had put them back to work during the Great Depression. Roosevelt denied Willkie's charge that he would lead the United States into war, and he accused the Republican of "playing politics with national defense." In reality, Roosevelt was playing politics too because he desperately wanted to aid

Britain, which was holding out against the bombs of the Luftwaffe, Hitler's air force.

Voters returned Roosevelt to office in the election of 1940. Secure in another term, the president felt confident enough to lead Americans toward a more active foreign policy. Just as Roosevelt had come under great pressure at home to keep the United States out of the war, the new British prime minister, Winston Churchill, was pleading with Roosevelt to come to Britain's aid.

The British people had charged Churchill with forming a government that would save Britain from the German assault. Roosevelt knew that the British Isles, isolated and running short of supplies, needed immediate help. Churchill was a persuasive man. His speeches stiffened the British resolve to ride out the German bombing raids, and his pleas to the American president made a profound impact. Churchill was an inspiring leader, and Roosevelt felt that the prime minister was the last guardian of democracy in Europe.

Arsenal of Democracy

Roosevelt came up with a plan to aid the British, which he announced at a White House press con-

Asking for help. British Prime Minister Winston Churchill (left) begged Roosevelt to come to his country's aid.

ference. According to his Lend-Lease Act, the United States would immediately provide Britain with war materials in exchange for later payments in goods or money. The scheme upheld the letter of the Neutrality Act but represented an unofficial alliance with the British. Roosevelt declared that the United States would act as the "arsenal of democracy."

Through Lend-Lease, American warships were handed over to the British Navy, and the United States received naval bases in return. Roosevelt had to show Congress that the United States was getting something out of the deal too; the acquisition of the British naval bases calmed the storm of criticism. In theory, all the U.S. aid to Britain was to be paid for, but the United States never asked for full repayment, and Britain made only token payments—in money, cases of Scotch whiskey, and other goods.

The effects of the Lend-Lease Act were felt immediately in the U.S. economy. Factories, closed for years during the Depression, reopened to meet the new demand for American war goods. "Manufacturers of watches, of farm implements, of linotypes and cash registers and automobiles and sewing machines and lawn mowers and locomotives are now making fuses and bomb packing crates and telescope mounts and shells and pistols and tanks," Roosevelt said in a fireside chat. Thanks to the British efforts against German aggression, the depression in the United States came to an end at last.

A Day of Infamy

One unseen effect of Roosevelt's Lend-Lease Act was that it tempted Germany to declare war on the United States. The Germans were outraged at the U.S. alliance with Britain. Nazi submarines began to hunt and destroy U.S. supply convoys headed for Britain.

To protect the Atlantic shipping routes, the U.S. Navy escorted the merchant ships. Roosevelt soon found himself conducting an undeclared war against Germany in the Atlantic Ocean. War with the Nazi regime seemed inevitable, when, out of the dawn skies over Hawaii, a new enemy struck the United States.

On Sunday morning, December 7, 1941, the bulk of the U.S. Pacific Fleet was anchored in Pearl Harbor, Hawaii. Just before 8 A.M., the officers and crew were going about their morning tasks, with no hint of the danger flying toward them. Their antiaircraft guns lay silent—ammunition locked up to prevent sabotage—when Japanese fighter-bombers appeared in the skies above.

Not expecting trouble, spotters assumed the planes were American so they took little notice. Suddenly, the ships' decks began to explode with

Surprise attack. Japanese aircraft bombed American ships at Pearl Harbor on December 7, 1941.

gunfire, as the Japanese planes unloaded on the U.S. fleet. The sky filled with thick black smoke, and the twisted and burned battleships keeled over and sank in the harbor. By 10 A.M., the fleet was reduced to a pile of burned-out hulks, and 2,388 U.S. sailors lay in watery graves in the Pacific.

The nation had been caught completely by surprise. A dreadful pall fell over the country as the

American people realized that they had just been attacked by the Japanese.

The next day, Roosevelt took his message to Congress. If the Japanese wanted a war, they would have one. "I ask that the Congress declare," he said to a packed room, "that since the unprovoked and dastardly attack by Japan on Sunday, December 7, 1941, a state of war has existed between the United States and the Japanese Empire." He soberly described the day of the attack as "a date which will live in infamy."

An Unholy Alliance

The Allied powers—which included Britain, France, and the Soviet Union, among others—were relieved to hear of the U.S. entry into World War II. But the United States was hardly prepared to throw itself into a global war. Much of its fleet lay at the bottom of Pearl Harbor. Its army had shrunk during the years of isolation from foreign affairs. The country needed time to get ready.

The war was not going to wait for the United States, however. Germany, united with Austria, had conquered all of western Europe. It had allied itself with Italy and Japan in what Roosevelt called an "unholy alliance." The three countries—Germany, Italy, and Japan—became known as the Axis powers.

The Axis powers delivered a stunning series of defeats to the Allies in the early years of the war. The Germans attacked the Soviet Union, and the Russians retreated into the vast steppes of Russia, unable to halt the advance. In Asia, the Japanese had taken over the British colonies of Hong Kong, Singapore, and Malaysia. They soon drove the Americans out of military bases in the Philippines. As U.S. General Douglas MacArthur, who was acting

Rejecting defeat. U.S. General Douglas MacArthur declared he would return to the Philippines after being driven out by the Japanese.

Franklin Delano Roosevelt: U.S. President

commander, left the islands with his troops, he made his famous pledge, "I shall return."

The Home Front

At home, Roosevelt mobilized the country. Millions of American men were drafted. Boot camps pumped out soldiers faster than they could arm them. The military was so ill prepared for war that many of the new soldiers had to train with broomsticks.

As America's men left for war, Roosevelt asked the country's women to take over the jobs the men had left behind—driving trucks, working on factory floors, and welding battleships in the nation's shipyards. Propaganda films showed the new American woman, her hair tied in a bandanna and a wrench in one hand. In posters and other printed propaganda, working women were represented by Rosie the Riveter, the ideal wartime woman, with a smudge of grease on her smiling face.

The country reached full employment, and U.S. industries reached production levels that startled even the most ambitious factory managers. The entry of women into the workforce created a dramatic social shift. Their participation in hard physical work was not only accepted, it was applauded.

Rosie the Riveter. Women all over the country took on factory jobs while men fought in World War II.

The social changes were far-reaching. Despite fierce opposition from the armed services, Roosevelt attempted to integrate African-Americans into the army. Roosevelt knew that they could make an important contribution to the war effort—which they did, despite the racist attacks they had to endure in the ranks.

Japanese Americans did not fare as well. After the attack on Pearl Harbor, America's hatred of "treacherous Japs" came to a boil. Mobs of angry people assaulted Japanese Americans, destroying their homes and property. Fear of Japanese-American spies and saboteurs created an environment of fear in California. Without considering the effects of his actions, Roosevelt approved the roundup of Japanese Americans and their imprisonment in camps. Japanese-American men could avoid the camps by enlisting in the army, and many did. Women, children, the elderly—and men who refused to fight for a country that had just arrested them—sat out the war in detention camps.

German Americans, who made up a large portion of the population of the Midwest and other parts of the country, were not imprisoned. In fact,

German-American Dwight D. Eisenhower became one of America's great leaders during this war.

Fighting Back

From Britain, General Eisenhower planned Operation Torch, the invasion of North Africa. Germany's Afrika Corps, commanded by General Erwin Rommel—known as the Desert Fox—was chewing up the British and threatening their hold on Egypt. Egypt was vital to the British because of the Suez Canal, through which Allied supplies were shipped to British India. The Americans agreed to open their counterstrike in the deserts of North Africa.

Soon, 35,000 Americans shipped out for French Morocco. The British were astounded at the technological efficiency of the Americans and impressed by their new weapons—tanks, artillery guns, and aircraft. The Americans were still novices on the battlefield, however, and took a pummeling. General Eisenhower later said that, after brooding over these disastrous early defeats, he decided he would never stop smiling again. He had learned a trick from Roosevelt—inspiring confidence in others through cheer, even when all looked hopeless.

From the White House, Roosevelt coordinated the grand strategy for the U.S. forces, but he left the fighting to his generals. Like the Germans, the Americans were fighting on two fronts: Churchill had secured their aid in Europe, but the Americans also had a score to settle with the Japanese. As soon as a shipyard christened a new warship, it set sail for the Pacific. Roosevelt closely followed the island-hopping campaign from his map rooms in Washington.

American warships fought with the Japanese at sea, and U.S. Marines engaged in ferocious land battles on Japanese-occupied Pacific islands. The Japanese soldiers showed great resistance and often fought to the death, but, by the summer of 1942, the Americans had begun to drive back the Japanese.

The Big Three

As American industries continued to pump out war supplies, Roosevelt extended the Lend-Lease Act to include Russia, China, and other countries. American forces and machinery were engaged all over the globe. By late 1942, the German advance had been halted in Russia and North Africa, and the Japanese were losing ground in the Pacific.

Roosevelt spent much time trying to hold the Allies together. Although he saw eye to eye with Churchill, coordinating goals and strategy with the British and the Russians tested even Roosevelt's diplomatic skills.

At the end of 1943, in the Iranian capital of Tehran, the three Allied leaders—Churchill, Roosevelt,

The Big Three. Joseph Stalin (left), Roosevelt (center), and Winston Churchill (right) met in Tehran.

and Joseph Stalin of the Soviet Union—met for the first time. Each of the three men, named The Big Three by the press, was arguing for his own country's interests. The brooding Russian leader, with his bristling mustache, demanded that the Allies open a second front outside Russia. Churchill reminded Stalin that the British had been fighting in North Africa and Asia for several years. He felt Stalin's remarks belittled the sacrifices that the British had already made in the war.

Roosevelt, looking confident in his pinstripe suit, believed that he could smooth over the other men's differences through the force of his own personality. Although he could not overcome Churchill's irritation, he did secure a promise from Stalin that Russia would enter the war in Asia, and the three leaders together outlined a plan for the invasion of Europe.

Operation Overlord

The invasion of Europe was called Operation Overlord by the Allied planners. It began on June 6, 1944, which later became known as D-Day.

The largest invasion fleet ever assembled landed that day on the beaches of Normandy in northwest

D-Day. The Allied troops landed on the beaches of Normandy and invaded France on June 14, 1944.

France. Allied planes bombed the German gun emplacements in an attempt to weaken resistance throughout the landing zone. But when the troops hit the beaches, they were met with withering enemy fire. Many Allied soldiers died before they ever reached the beaches—shot down while wading to shore. Within minutes, the beaches were littered with bodies—but by day's end, the Allies had gained a foothold in Europe.

Over the next few weeks, Allied troops advanced into France. Commandos were dropped by plane behind enemy lines to harass the Germans. French villagers welcomed the Allied soldiers as they passed through western France on their way to Paris.

My Little Dog, Fala

Roosevelt was in high spirits. American forces were winning victories in Europe and in the Pacific. Only politics intruded on the moment—four years had passed and it was time for another election. Even in the middle of a world war, the people must have their say.

Roosevelt showed signs of strain during the presidential campaign of 1944. His health had been failing for some time, and even his periodic visits to the baths at Warm Springs had not completely revived him. His opponent, Governor Thomas Dewey of New York, raised doubts about Roosevelt's health. Always spurred on by a good political fight, Roosevelt began a tour of the country. Expertly playing the role of statesman and commander in chief, he made his bid for a fourth term. Having wrestled with such iron-willed men as Stalin and Churchill, Roosevelt was not going to be defeated by an upstart like Dewey.

Roosevelt had already been in office for twelve years, and many U.S. soldiers were too young to remember ever having anyone else as president. Dewey leveled all the old charges, however, reminding people that Roosevelt had been the only man ever to serve a third term—and now he was asking for a fourth.

In a speech before the Teamsters Union, Roosevelt showed signs of the good humor he was famous for. The spark was back, and so, too, was the jovial fighting spirit. Responding to a comment made about his Scottish terrier, Fala, Roosevelt became indignant against his Republican critics. "These Republican leaders have not been content with attacks on me, or my wife, or on my sons. No, not content with that they now include my little dog Fala. Well, of course, I don't resent attacks, and my

A man and his dog. Roosevelt joked about the comments made regarding Fala, his Scottish terrier.

family doesn't resent attacks, but Fala *does* resent them."

On election night, Roosevelt ate his "lucky" dinner, scrambled eggs, and listened to the results come in over the radio. By morning, Roosevelt learned that he had become the first, and last, president in American history to be elected for a fourth term.

A Lasting Peace

On a frigid January day, Roosevelt delivered his last inaugural address, which was less than five minutes long. "We have learned to be citizens of the world," he said. The country had suffered greatly, and Roosevelt saw no need to make a rambling speech.

Roosevelt's last great dream as president was to secure some arrangement between the Allies to ensure peace after the war. He sailed to the Russian port city of Yalta for a last meeting with The Big Three. The Allies were closing in on Berlin, the German capital. Roosevelt convinced Churchill that the Russians should have the honor of taking the city, because the Russians had suffered more losses than any other Allied country.

Churchill was suspicious of Russian intentions in Eastern Europe, however. He suspected—rightly—that the Russians would not leave the region after the war. To Churchill, replacing the Germans with the Russians seemed like exchanging one form of tyranny for another.

His efforts to mediate discussions between the two men exhausted Roosevelt. Deep lines showed in his face, and black circles had settled permanently under his eyes. He left Yalta feeling that he had worked out an arrangement between the leaders, but strengthening the alliance had been as exhausting as waging the war.

When Roosevelt returned to the United States, he visited Warm Springs for some much-needed rest. While at the spa, Roosevelt showed none of his old vigor. He no longer resembled the laughing man who had once paddled around the pools. On April 12, 1945, only three months into his fourth term, Roosevelt complained of a headache. Two hours later, he was dead.

When news of the president's death was broadcast over the radio, grown men and women wept in the streets. Roosevelt had been president for so long

The funeral at Hyde Park. Franklin Delano Roosevelt died before World War II ended, but his work for world peace continued.

that Americans couldn't imagine anyone else in the White House. The broad-smiling man with the upturned cigarette holder and tiny spectacles, the man whose spirit had carried them through the Great Depression and led them in battle was gone.

The Fighting Ends

At the end of April, Allied forces closed in on Berlin. The German city lay in ruins from round-the-clock bombing raids. Even though there was nothing left to defend, fanatical Nazis fought among the rubble of their capital. When they reached Hitler's underground bunker, Allied soldiers discovered his body. He had committed suicide rather than face the humiliation of capture.

War in the Pacific lasted until August 1945. On August 6 and August 9, President Harry Truman had destroyed the Japanese cities of Hiroshima and Nagasaki with a terrifying new weapon—the atomic bomb. The Japanese surrendered on August 14. For the first time in more than six years, the world was finally at peace.

Although Roosevelt did not live to see it, the League of Nations that he fought so hard for—the alliance of countries that would prevent future wars—reemerged as the United Nations in October 1945. Roosevelt himself had coined the name *United Nations.* In January 1946, his wife, Eleanor, attended the first session. This international peacekeeping organization still exists today, and almost every country in the world is a member.

TIMELINE

1882   Franklin Delano Roosevelt born on January 30 in Hyde Park, New York

1896   Enters the Groton School in Connecticut

1900   Graduates from Groton and enrolls at Harvard College in Cambridge, Massachusetts

1903   Becomes engaged to a distant cousin named Anna Eleanor Roosevelt

1905   Marries Eleanor and enrolls at Columbia University's law school in New York City

1907   Passes the New York State bar examination; leaves Columbia without a degree for a job at a law firm

1906   Eleanor gives birth to daughter Anna

1907   Eleanor gives birth to son James

1909   The Roosevelts' third child, Franklin Jr., dies at the age of eighteen months

1910   Wins a seat in the New York state legislature

1913   Is appointed assistant secretary of the U.S. Navy

1919   Observes Treaty of Versailles, a peace conference held outside of Paris, France, at which the League of Nations is created

1920	Runs for vice president of the United States on a Democratic ticket with James M. Cox of Ohio
1921	Is stricken with polio and loses the use of both legs
1927	Establishes the Georgia Warm Springs Foundation for polio sufferers
1928	Becomes governor of New York
1932	Is elected president of the United States
1933	Congress enacts President Roosevelt's New Deal programs to help speed up the country's economy recovery
1935	Signs the American Neutrality Act, a pledge to keep the United States out of World War II, and the Social Security Act, a bill establishing pensions for retired citizens
1936	Is reelected president of the United States
1940	Is reelected for an unprecedented third term as president of the United States
1943	Meets with Winston Churchill of Britain and Joseph Stalin of the Soviet Union for the first time in the Iranian capital of Tehran; the three leaders outline a plan for the invasion of Europe
1944	Is reelected for a fourth term as president of the United States
1945	Has last meeting with Churchill and Stalin at Yalta; dies in Warm Springs, Georgia, on April 12

Franklin Delano Roosevelt: U.S. President

HOW TO BECOME A GOVERNMENT OFFICIAL

The Job

Federal and state officials hold positions in the legislative, executive, and judicial branches of government at the state and national levels. They include governors, judges, senators, representatives, and the president and vice president of the country. Government officials are responsible for preserving the government against external and domestic threats. They also supervise and resolve conflicts between private and public interest, regulate the economy, protect the political and social rights of the citizens, and provide goods and services. Officials may, among other things, pass laws, set up social-service programs, and decide how to spend the taxpayers' money.

Think about the last time you cast a vote, such as in a school election. How did you make your decision? Was it based on the personal qualities of the candidate? The positions of the candidate? Certain issues of importance to

113

you? As voters, we choose carefully when electing a government official, taking many things into consideration. Whether we're electing a new governor and lieutenant governor for the state, a president and vice president for the country, or senators and representatives for the state legislature or the U.S. Congress, we're choosing people to act on our behalf. The decisions of state and federal lawmakers affect your daily life and your future. State and federal officials pass laws that affect the arts, education, taxes, employment, health care, and other areas in efforts to change and improve communities and standards of living.

Nearly every state's governing body resembles that of the federal government. Just as the U.S. Congress is composed of the Senate and the House of Representatives, every state except Nebraska has a senate and a house. The president and vice president head the executive branch of the U.S. government, while the states elect governors and lieutenant governors. The governor is the chief executive officer of a state. In all states, a large group of officials handle agriculture, highway and motor-vehicle supervision, public safety and corrections, regulation of intrastate business and industry, and some aspects of education, public health, and welfare. The governor's job is to oversee their work. Some states also have a lieutenant governor, who serves as the presiding officer of the state's senate. Other elected officials commonly include a secretary of state, state treasurer, state auditor, attorney general, and superintendent of public instruction.

Besides the president and vice president of the United States, the executive branch of the national government consists of the president's cabinet. The cabinet includes the secretaries of state, treasury, defense, interior, agriculture, and health and human services. These officials are appointed by the president and approved by the Senate. The members of the Office of Management and Budget, the Council of Economic Advisors, and the National Security Council are also executive officers of the national government.

State senators and state representatives are elected to represent various districts and regions of cities and counties within the state. The number of members in a state's legislature varies from state to state. The U.S. Congress has 100 senators as established by the Constitution—2 senators from each state—and 435 representatives. (The number of representatives is based on a state's population—California has the highest number of representatives with 52.) The primary job of all legislators, on both the state and national levels, is to make laws. With a staff of assistants, senators and representatives learn as much as they can about the bills being considered. They research legislation, prepare reports, meet with constituents and interest groups, speak to the press, and discuss legislation on the floor of the House or Senate. Legislators also may be involved in selecting other members of the government, supervising the government administration, gathering and spending money, impeaching executive and judicial officials, and setting up election procedures, among other activities.

Requirements

High School Courses in government, civics, and history will help you gain an understanding of the structure of state and federal governments. English courses are also important. You need good writing skills to communicate with your constituents and other government officials. Math and accounting will help you develop the analytical skills needed to understand statistics and demographics. Science courses will help you make decisions concerning health, medicine, and technological advances. Journalism classes will help you learn about the media and the role they play in politics.

Postsecondary State and federal legislators come from all walks of life. Some hold master's degrees and doctorates, while others have only high-school educations. Although most government officials hold law degrees, others have undergraduate or graduate degrees in such areas as journalism, economics, political science, history, and English. No matter what you majored in as an undergraduate, you'll likely be required to take classes in English literature, statistics, foreign language, Western civilization, and economics. Graduate students concentrate more on one area of study; some prospective government officials pursue a master's degree in public administration or international affairs. Take part in your college's internship program, which will involve you with local and state officials, or pursue your own internship opportunities. By contacting the offices of your state legislators and your state's members of Congress, you can apply for internships directly.

Other Requirements

Good "people skills" will help you make connections, gain election, and make things happen once you are in office. You should also enjoy argument, debate, and opposition—you'll get a lot of it as you attempt to get laws passed. A calm temperament in such situations will earn the respect of your colleagues. Strong character and a good background will help you avoid the personal attacks that occasionally accompany government office.

Exploring

A person as young as sixteen years old can gain experience with legislature. The U.S. Congress, and possibly your own state legislature, has opportunities for teenagers to work as pages. They want young people who have demonstrated a commitment to government study. If you work for Congress, you'll be running messages across Capitol Hill, and you'll have the opportunity to see senators and representatives debating and discussing bills. The length of a page's service can be from one summer to one year. Contact your state's senator or representative for an application.

Become involved with local elections. Many candidates for local and state offices welcome young people to assist with campaigns. You'll make calls, post signs, and get to see a candidate at work. You'll also meet others with an interest in government, and your experience will help you gain a more prominent role in later campaigns.

Employers

State legislators work for the state government, but due to the part-time nature of some legislative offices they may hold part-time jobs or own their own businesses. Federal officials work full-time for the Senate, the House, or the executive branch.

Starting Out

There is no direct career path for state and federal officials. Some stumble into their positions after some success with political activism on the grassroots level. Others work their way up from local government positions to state legislature and then into federal office. Those who serve in the U.S. Congress have worked in the military, journalism, academics, business, and many other fields.

Advancement

Initiative is one key to success in politics. Advancement can be rapid for someone who is a fast learner and is independently motivated, but a career in politics usually takes a long time to establish. Most state and federal officials start by pursuing training and work experience in their particular field, while getting involved in politics at the local level. Many people progress from local politics to state politics. It is not uncommon for a state legislator to eventually run for a seat in Congress. Appointees to the president's cabinet and presidential and vice presidential candidates have frequently held positions in Congress.

Work Environment

Most government officials work in a typical office setting. Some may work a regular 40-hour week, while others work long hours and weekends. One potential drawback to political life, particularly for the candidate running for office, is that there is no real off-duty time. The individual is continually under observation by the press and public, and the personal lives of candidates and officeholders are discussed frequently in the media.

Because these officials must be appointed or elected in order to keep their jobs, it is difficult to plan for long-range job objectives. There may be long periods of unemployment, when living off savings or working at other jobs may be necessary.

Frequent travel is involved in campaigning and in holding office. People with children may find this lifestyle demanding on their families.

Earnings

In general, salaries for government officials tend to be lower than salaries in the private sector. For state legislators, the pay can be very much lower. According to the National Conference of State Legislatures, state legislators make $10,000 to $47,000 a year. A few states, however, don't pay state legislators anything but an expense allowance. And even those legislators who receive a salary may not receive any benefits. However, a state's top officials are paid better: The Book of the States lists salaries of state governors as ranging from $60,000 to $130,000.

The Congressional Research Service publishes the salaries and benefits of Congress members. Senators and representatives are paid $136,673 annually. Congress members are entitled to a cost-of-living increase every year but don't always accept it. Congressional leaders such as the Speaker of the House and the Senate majority leader receive higher salaries than other Congress members. For example, the Speaker of the House makes $171,500 a year. Also, U.S. Congress members receive excellent insurance, vacation, and other benefits.

Outlook

To attract more candidates for legislative offices, states may consider salary increases and better benefits for state senators and representatives. But changes in pay and benefits for federal officials are unlikely. An increase in the number of representatives is possible as the U.S. population grows, but it would require additional office space and other costly expansions. For the most part, the structures of state and federal legislatures will remain unchanged, although the topic of limiting the number of terms a representative is allowed to serve often arises in election years.

The federal government has made efforts to shift costs to the states. If this trend continues, it could change the way state legislatures and executive officers operate in regards to public funding. Already, welfare reform has resulted in state governments looking for financial aid in handling welfare cases and job programs. Arts funding may also become the sole responsibility of the states as the National Endowment for the Arts loses support from Congress.

The government's commitment to developing a place on the Internet has made it easier to contact your state and federal representatives, learn about legislation, and organize a grassroots movement. This increase in voter awareness of candidates, public policy issues, and legislation may affect how future representatives make decisions. Also look for government programming to be part of cable television's expansion into digital broadcasting. New means of communication will involve voters even more in the actions of their representatives.

TO LEARN MORE ABOUT GOVERNMENT OFFICIALS

Books

Bonner, Mike. *How to Become an Elected Official.* Broomall, Penn.: Chelsea House, 2000.

Fish, Bruce, and Becky Durost Fish. *The History of the Democratic Party.* Broomall, Penn.: Chelsea House, 2000.

James, Lesley. *Women in Government: Politicians, Lawmakers, Law Enforcers.* Austin, Tex.: Raintree/Steck-Vaughn, 2000.

Lutz, Norma Jean. *The History of the Republican Party.* Broomall, Penn.: Chelsea House, 2000.

Websites

Congress.Org

http://www.congress.org/

A guide to Congress, providing information about House and Senate members as well as current bills and legislation

U.S. House of Representatives

http://www.house.gov
Provides a variety of information about the House of Representatives

U.S. Senate

http://www.senate.gov
Information about senators and how the Senate works

Where to Write
U.S. Senate

Office of Senator (Name)
United States Senate
Washington, DC 20515
202/224-3121

U.S. House of Representatives

Washington, DC 20515
202/224-3121

National Conference of State Legislatures

1560 Broadway, Suite 700
Denver, CO 80202
303/830-2200
For information about *State Legislatures Magazine*, and other information concerning state legislatures

TO LEARN MORE ABOUT FRANKLIN DELANO ROOSEVELT

Books

Freedman, Russell. *Franklin Delano Roosevelt.* New York: Clarion Books, 1992.

Morris, Jeffrey. *The FDR Way.* Minneapolis, Minn.: Lerner Publications, 1996.

Schuman, Michael A. *Franklin D. Roosevelt: The Four-Term President.* Springfield, N.J.: Enslow Publishers, 1996.

Websites

New Deal Network

http://newdeal.feri.org

An educational guide to the Great Depression

Time and the Presidency
*http://www.pathfinder.com/offers/presidents/preview_roo
sevelt.html*
Biographical information about FDR

Interesting Places to Visit
Museum of Franklin D. Roosevelt Library
4079 Albany Post Road
Hyde Park, New York 12538
845/229-8114
Exhibits geared towards children and young adults K–12

The White House
1600 Pennsylvania Avenue, N.W.
Washington, D.C. 20502
202/456-7041

INDEX

Page numbers in *italics* indicate illustrations.

ABOUT THE AUTHOR

Robert Green holds an M.A. in Journalism from New York University and a B.A. in English literature from Boston University. He has written sixteen other books including a biography of John Glenn in the Ferguson Career Biographies and biographies of Alexander the Great, Tutankhamen, Julius Caesar, Hannibal, Herod the Great, and Cleopatra, as well as biographies of six British monarchs. He has also written a book on China for young adults as well as *"Vive La France": The French Resistance During World War II* and *Dictators of the Modern World*. He lives in New York City.